HOSANNA!

Horn in F

Arranged by Walter H. Barnes
Slowly ♩=72-80

.lestrina
25-1594)

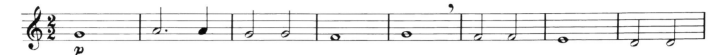

NON NOBIS DOMINE

Horn in F

Arranged by Walter H. Barnes
Smoothly ♩=84

William Byrd
(ca. 1540-1623)

AH, HOLY JESUS
(Herzliebster Jesu)

Horn in F

Arranged by Richard Walters

Johannes Crüger
(1598-1662)

WHEN JESUS WEPT

Horn in F

Arranged by Charles Sayre

Slowly, and Sustained *(♩ = 92)

William Billings
(1746-1800)

*Legato throughout

KITTERY

Horn in F

Arranged by Charles Sayre

William Billings
(1746-1800)

17 COLLECTED EASY QUINTETS

THE CANADIAN BRASS

HAL•LEONARD®

ETERNAL FATHER, STRONG TO SAVE
(Melita)

Horn in F

Arranged by Richard Walters

John B. Dykes
(1823-1876)

VICTORIOUS LOVE
(Amor Vittorioso)

Horn in F

Arranged by Charles Sayre

Giovanni Giacomo Gastoldi
(ca. 1554-1609)

Play through the piece twice.

IN THE HALL OF THE MOUNTAIN KING
from *Peer Gynt*

Horn in F

Arranged by Charles Sayre

Edvard Grieg
(1843-1907)

MENUET
from *Music for the Royal Fireworks*

Horn in F

Arranged by Walter H. Barnes

George Frideric Handel
(1685-1759)

O SACRED HEAD
(O Haupt voll Blut und Wunden)

orn in F

Harmonization by Johann Sebastian Bach
Arranged by Charles Sayre

Hans Leo Hassler
(1564-1612)

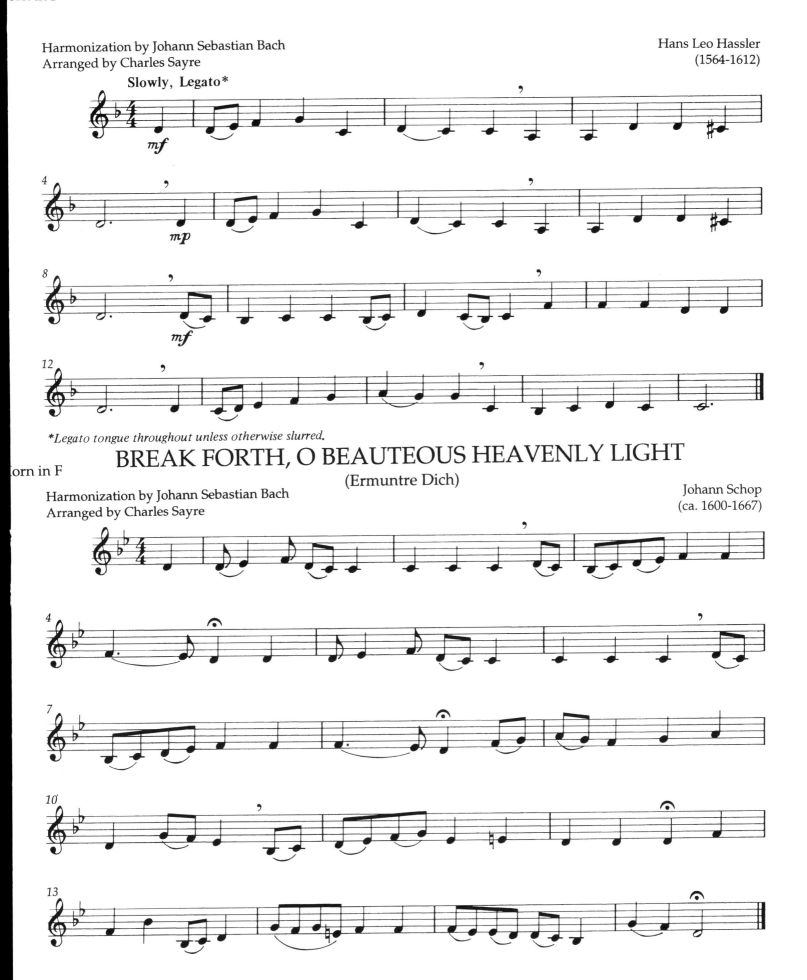

Legato tongue throughout unless otherwise slurred.

BREAK FORTH, O BEAUTEOUS HEAVENLY LIGHT
(Ermuntre Dich)

orn in F

Harmonization by Johann Sebastian Bach
Arranged by Charles Sayre

Johann Schop
(ca. 1600-1667)

AUSTRIAN HYMN

from String Quartet No. 62 "Emperor" in C Major, Op. 76, No. 3

Horn in F

Arranged by Charles Sayre

Franz Joseph Haydn
(1732-1809)

A MIGHTY FORTRESS
(Ein feste Burg ist unser Gott)

Horn in F

Arranged by Richard Walters

Martin Luther
(1483-1546)

CANON

Horn in F

Arranged by Charles Sayre

Thomas Tallis
(ca. 1505-1585)

BEAUTIFUL SAVIOR
(Schönster Herr Jesu)
from *Münster Gesangbuch*, 1677

Horn in F

Arranged by Richard Walters

Traditional

13

CHRIST THE LORD IS RISEN TODAY

from *Lyra Davidica*, 1708

Horn in F

Arranged by Richard Walters

Traditional

THE CANADIAN BRASS

CONTENTS

SCORE AND PARTS AVAILABLE SEPARATELY:

Conductor's Score	50486953
Trumpet 1 in B-flat	50486948
Trumpet 2 in B-flat	50486949
Trombone	50486951
Tuba	50486952

ALSO AVAILABLE IN THIS SERIES:

14 Collected Intermediate Quintets	50486959

U.S. $8.99

HL50486950

HAL•LEONARD®
CORPORATION
7777 W. BLUEMOUND RD. P.O. BOX 13819 MILWAUKEE, WI 53213

www.canbrass.com
www.halleonard.com

ISBN 978-1-4234-8311-3

WE GATHER TOGETHER
(Kremser)

Horn in F

Arranged by Richard Walters

Traditional